First Printing 2021

ISBN: 9798486177866

CW00557748

'An impassioned and vital call to arms for women everywhere.'

— E. L. Williams, author of 'The First Ethereal'

Shine Your Light Goddess, Shine Your Light

I dedicate this book to all the amazing Shining Beings of Light who are about to read these words, they are written for you with love in my heart. I hope you get what you need right now in this moment from the information that is about to flow. I hope that you uncover some old shit, release it, and let it go, so that you can step forward and Shine YOUR Light so brightly in this world. I dedicate this book to you indeed.

I also dedicate this book to my beautiful Feline Companion, my beautiful cat Isis, who passed away as we began our first live round of our first Shine Your Light Goddess, Shine Your Light Bootcamp. I miss her every day, and her Spirit very much lives on as she taught my 2 boy cats some terrible habits that make me smile and roll my eyes every time they do them.

My gratitude goes to all those amazing Women who have gone before me, my ancestors, my teachers – both in Spirit and in the flesh, my heartfelt gratitude goes to them indeed.

My gratitude goes to the beautiful Aishling Mooney who recommended Leonie Dawson's 'Get your book written already' course which has been the rocket up my arse that was required to sit and put the book that has been in my head for so long into words – thank you indeed dear one.

And heartfelt thanks to Leonie Dawson's 'write your book in 40 days' course. Any budding authors out there, buy the course, it's essentially Leonie saying 'Just write your fucking book' a zillion times, but it works! Thank you, Leonie!

My gratitude also goes to Hannah Liversidge, the beautiful soul who edited my first book 'A Love Letter To My Old Self, from Hamster Wheel to Happiness ™'. The stunning Hannah edited my book, sent it off to print, and forgot to put her own name in the foreword! So, I am putting it here so that my gratitude for Hannah's work is in writing!

Head to www.mynaturalhappiness.com and download a copy of that book for free, as a gift from my heart to yours.

And of course, my gratitude goes to the amazing editor of this book, thank you so much Dear Angie Brown. Thank you for stepping into this space with me, thank you.

Now before we begin, I would also like to tell you that I have an ongoing resistance to full stops! I know, it seems odd to some, but it is from memory that in my family, full stops were used when we are angry with someone, so when I am writing I don't put in the full stops. I am fully aware that it is not grammatically correct, and I know Angie has kept some in for me but literally had to remove the commas from the whole book.

So, enough on that for now, let us begin...

QR Code for www.mynaturalhappiness.com

Chapter 1

So, how does this tale begin? Back in June 2020, in between lockdown 1 and 2 here in the UK. That Summer that was supposed to mark the end of COVID19 lockdowns in our lives, although most of us knew it so wasn't going to be the end of it. During the window in time, that shifted so much for so many people, there was a real uprising of Feminine power and energy.

Women were calling for BALANCE, and Women were, and are getting louder and louder – tired of being branded 'unladylike' just for having a voice, Women were, and are getting louder.

Anyone who has been paying attention to the energy paradigms of the past few years will have seen it coming, and lockdown removed those invisible last few dregs of fears of being seen for SO MANY AMAZING WOMEN. Our time had come, and our excuses had been ripped away.

For too long there has been a huge imbalance in the world, for too long the world has been run by old fat men, with their 'schoolboy humour' and their boys clubs. The lack of compassion, empathy, thought, the lack of kindness in their decisions has been apparent everywhere.

Whilst so many male politicians around the world dithered and blustered their way through the pandemic, female politicians took decisive and quick action to protect their citizens – with kindness and compassion in their hearts – it shone through.

At a time when Women have had enough!!!!!!! So many Women in lockdown just said enough, is enough – it's time to balance this shit out and stepped forward to SHINE.

And so, in this melting pot of emotions, for the first time ever, in history, men stopped and listened.

For the first time ever, in history, men stopped and wondered if there is a better way of doing this?

Across the globe, the Women leaders were acting decisively, with compassion – no blundering, no going backwards and forwards – they were taking action quickly, effectively and getting things done.

And men LISTENED for the first time, men listened!

So, more and more Women stood up and talked. More and more Women shared their truths. More and more Women shared their experiences. More and more Women shared their stories.

And MEN listened, well some of them anyway.

So, maybe, just maybe the energy of the World is shifting already?

Maybe the lessons will be learnt, and maybe Men will listen, and maybe there will finally be a redress of the imbalance of the Male/Female energies across the world going forward. Finally!

… And maybe, just maybe there is more work to be done, more Women have work to do on shedding the shackles of their past and stepping into the future with no fear of recrimination. Shining their Lights so brightly in this world AND MAKING A BLOODY DIFFERENCE in this world, maybe indeed, maybe.

And so, I listened to the voices, back in that window of time between Lockdown 1 and Lockdown 2. Anyone with any aptitude of seeing into the future, whether it be from a scientific background, or a spiritual background could see, lockdown 2 was coming and it was going to be devastatingly deadly, harsh, horrid, and awful – and it was.

And, in that window of time, I stopped, I listened, I asked 'What can I do here, what can I do to contribute to this conversation? What can I do to help the female/male energies of this world?' What can I do?'

I listened to Spirit, to my Guides, to the Angels and the Ancestors, to the Goddesses and Gods, I listened with my heart, my body and my soul, I listened so intently,

And, Shine Your Light Goddess, Shine Your Light Bootcamp was born.

Literally channelled overnight.

I was given it all, by Spirit, by my Ancestors of Blood and Spirit, by my incredible Guides, by my animal spirits who walk with me. I was given this information and told I had to do the work myself AND invite others along for the ride!

I mean, there was no messing. I had to do this – and NOW, not later NOW.

I can still feel that insistence from them as I type. So strong! So there!

So, I did!

I mean, I have been teaching others for YEARS. I have run Retreats, Reiki Courses, Angel Courses, I created a yearlong programme to help others go from their Hamster Wheel to Happiness which is called the Seeds of Change Programme. I have helped SO MANY WOMEN with so many things in their life, for YEARS, and nothing has felt quite so insistent as this message that Spirit told me to SHOUT from the rooftops with.

Shine Your Light Goddess, Shine Your Light

Time to shed the shackles of the past and shine your light so brightly.

Time to balance out the female/male energies of this world.

Time to help Spiritual, Compassionate Women step forward, release their fears, release their shackles of the past. This life and past lives. Time to help them step forward and SHINE THEIR LIGHTS SO BRIGHTLY in this world.

So, they can make a bloody difference to the world!

So, they can climb the corporate ladder, or climb the charity sector ladder that is filled with old boys' networks. So that they can become more successful in their businesses. So that they can be more seen in these areas and more successful.

And become RICH.

Yeah, I said it. Doing this work will help you succeed in your endeavours, which in turn will help you become RICH beyond your wildest dreams.

And then you will have MONEY to make a difference in this world, and like it or lump it, money talks.

And when Women have Money, it tends to get spent on different things.

Building schools
Building Libraries
Planting Forests
Supporting Foodbanks
Providing medical care in places who need it most across the globe
Giving to charity

As I sit here, MacKenzie Scott, Jeff Bezos ex-wife has just given away 2.7 billion USD to charities she supports. Two point seven billion dollars. Let that sink in a little.

Two point seven billion dollars.

Just imagine the difference that money is going to make to so many peoples' lives!

So, yeah, I think it's time Women (I am very much including myself here!) stood up, are seen and heard in this world, make a difference, get paid well for it, and redress the balance of power and wealth in this world. Like it or not, money talks and the wealthier women are, the more compassionate voices there are doing the talking, financially speaking, in this world.

When Women step forward and release their fears, when they step forward in this world and Shine their Lights so brightly, even with that residual 'oh shit, this feels a little scary' voice in their heads, when Women step forward and are SEEN by the people who they want to be seen by – when Women step forward and SHINE their Lights so BRIGHTLY, SO many AMAZING things happen!!

When they ALLOW themselves to RECEIVE the abundance of the world, energy wise, financially, love, when they allow themselves to receive, SO much goodness flows!!

And we ALL have a part to play, we ALL have a voice here, we can ALL contribute to this conversation.

The more the merrier! The more the better. Old school patriarchy business phrases like 'Crush the competition' and 'Be the top of the game' and 'There can only be one winner in this' have been replaced by phrases such as: -

'There is room for us all'
'The more the merrier'
'This is a team game'
'We are in this together'
'A rising tide lifts all boats'
'We have totally got this'
'Joining the conversation'

I could go on...

Language is shifting. Women are stepping forward. Women across the world are saying enough is enough.

Women are making a huge difference to this world.

Spoiler alert here: YOU have been called too, by reading this book, you have been called too. You –have been asked to share your story and your gifts with the world. You have been offered a seat at this table. By picking up this book and reading it, you, dear reader, Dear Goddess, YOU have been called to add your voice to the cacophony of voices that is chiming across the world right now. Whether you read this the day the book is published or ten, twenty, forty or fifty years from now you, dear reader, Dear Goddess, you have been called, you have been invited to share your story, to share your gifts, you have been called too.

Will you accept the invitation?

That part is up to you.

You have been invited, wholeheartedly to this conversation – to this party.

Exactly as you are.

Because you, Dear Goddess, are bloody amazing, exactly as you are. You are blinking beautiful, inside and out, and YOU have so much to offer, so much to share. Your story, your voice is so needed in the world right now, and the world is listening.

Are you ready to speak?

Are there fears to overcome?

Is there a voice inside saying, 'It's not safe?' 'It's too scary' 'Watch your back' 'Be careful!' 'Keep your protection up at MAX HERE'?

All of that?

Right?

That's where the Shine Your Light Goddess, Shine Your Light Bootcamp came in.

That's what I was told by Spirit to bring to the table.

For generations, Women HID from the world, they had to!

Time to Shine Goddess, it is your time to Shine Dear One.

Do these words resonate with you?

Are you a Woman of Spirit who has been resisting shining your light in this world? Are you still hiding? Does your head WANT you to succeed, however something inside of you is holding you back? Keeping you in the shadows?

It is NOT your fault! As Women of Spirit, we have been hiding for YEARS! For GENERATIONS in fact!

We had to, to avoid persecution in times gone by, to avoid being bullied – we have been taught for centuries to 'hide in plain sight' in order to go undetected as we move through this world.

We will keep hiding until our Soul, our Ancestors, all those in our Spiritual Lineage, feel SAFE enough to SHINE! I did the same, I HID for years until I realised this. You CAN do the work to feel safe enough to SHINE in this world. Imagine what you will achieve when you shine your light out there? Imagine what the Generations to come, in your Spiritual Lineage, will achieve knowing they are safe enough to SHINE? The possibilities are truly endless.

My Shine Your Light Goddess, Shine Your Light Bootcamp is a beautiful 8-week journey to release the shackles of the past, so you can step forward in this world and SHINE. In this book, I will talk you through the steps, in such a safe space, so that you can start the process of releasing those shackles, unlocking your potential, one nugget at a time,

There is always work to do, there is always more stuff than we realise, so, there is a complimentary workbook to download and print off available here so you can journal and make notes as you read.

https://my-natural-happiness.newzenler.com/f/shine-your-light-goddess-shine-your-light-the-workbook

QR code for the workbook

"Just write your fucking book"

Leonie Dawson

Chapter 2

Please know that some of these tools, some of these techniques may resonate with you now, and some may not, but that is ok!

Work with what works for you. I am not asking you to complete everything. I am not asking you to do anything that does not align with you & your heart. All I am asking is that you stay open and playfully curious, to the information that is about to flow your way.

It might change your life, it might not, it might uncover so much for you, it might not. Just stay in curiosity and release any judgements, and please, please, do not beat yourself up if you do not complete every single sheet of the workbook.

Just reading this book may be enough for you to make a huge shift right now, that could be all you need!

If this book uncovers old memories that you find hard to handle, that you want outside help with, please, please, please, go find the right help for you with that issue. There are thousands of amazing therapists and coaches. Thousands of amazing souls out there to help you. Please, please, release any self-judgement on asking for help. It is a whole lot easier when you reach out and ask for help, I promise you that!

And of course, if this starts a ball rolling and you want to go deeper, come join the bootcamp and play with us.

You are invited, and you are so welcome, just head to this link and find out more.

https://my-natural-happiness.newzenler.com/courses/shine-your-light-goddess-shine-your-light

QR code for course enrolment

"The thing you are seeking is also seeking you"

Ivanla Vanzant

Chapter 3

Let's clear the shit so that we can release the crap and shine our lights brightly in this world.

I want to invite you to think about your big dream, the one that you have been harbouring for years, the one you may or may not have told people in the past, that big dream in your heart, no matter how deep or shallow it is, no judgements here – just think about your big dream.

Ask yourself the questions:

- 'Why have I held back on being seen in this world?'

- "What has stopped me taking the steps to achieve my big dream?

- 'What has stopped me making waves where I have wanted to?'

It is so time consuming hanging onto this stuff that might come up for you. It is so draining, and I know it feels comfortable to hang onto it, I know it feels as if it is protecting you, but it's not. It might have done when you were 5 years old and facing the school bully, but it's not now. It is just getting in the way of you taking the steps to achieve your dreams.

Total side note: if bullying came up, and if you are being bullied in the workplace, call them out, report the bully to HR. Be the person who takes that stand for you and for others there. You are not aged 5 anymore, and we are not living in the 1970's. So, call them out and make the workplace nicer for everyone.

Let's get back to the questions.

- Why have you been holding back from being seen in this world?

- Have you been bullied?

- Are you afraid to be seen?

- Are you afraid you will be laughed at?

- So many people who I have served over the years have uncovered so much by just sitting down in meditation and asking their Guides this question.

- Are you afraid of being successful?

- Are you afraid of what others might think?

- Are you scared you will upset the status quo at home?

- Are you afraid you might outshine your family?

- Are you afraid you might outshine your other half?

- Are you afraid you might earn more than those you love?

- What is it that has kept you from shining your light and taking the steps that will help you make such amazing waves in this world,

- How is it serving you? How is it impacting your life now?

- Is it really worth hanging on to?

I have got some tougher love for you. It really is not. You are reading this because the Universe has prompted you to let go of this shit already.

It is time to heal this shit.

It is time to let it go. Let it fall to floor so that this shit becomes manure to plant your roses. It's your time to shine and you are so, so, so ready.

So, how do you release this? There are so many tools that can work. My two favourite tools to work with are so simple.

Forgive that shit. Release it! To coin a phrase let it fucking go already. Forgive and release the energy attached to it, it is no longer serving you.

Tap some love into your being "Even though I am scared to be seen, I deeply and completely love and accept myself" (just do a YouTube search for tapping (EFT – Emotional Freedom technique), and you will so many tutorials).

If you allow yourself to look to the future, to your future where this stuff has been released out of your energy fields, you may see that it is so worth doing.

What will your life look like after you have released this energy? What will your life feel like? What will you get on your soapbox and shout about? What messages, stories, healings will YOU share with the world once you have released the fear of being seen.

REALLY feel into this dream work. What are your possibilities AFTER you have let go of that energy? What will you choose to fill that space up? What will that FEEL like? What will you ACHIEVE and SHARE with the world?

Once you really feel into the possibilities, it is so much easier to release, as you realise it is time to let it go already. It is safe for you to shine. It is your time, and you are so ready.

Simples, right? If the answer is no and you want more support around it, come and join the bootcamp! The invitation for you is right here!

https://my-natural-happiness.newzenler.com/courses/shine-your-light-goddess-shine-your-light

QR code for course enrolment

"Sometimes saying no to others is about saying yes to yourself, and it's safe for you to do this"

Kate Arbuckle

Chapter 4

Let's go into the Ancestral Work.

As I have said before, there might be so much to let go of within our Ancestral Line. Some of it was there for a reason, to protect our Female Ancestors from literally being burnt at the stake, and some has no business being there. Well actually, on reflection from writing these words, having to stay silent so that you were not burnt at the stake has no business being there as the act of being burnt at the stake should never have been there in the first place, let's get real here.

Sacrificing Women at the stake, for the purposes of egotistical men feeling more comfortable in themselves? Nope, nope, nope and nope.

And we are where we are.

Some of these women were so powerful it scared men. It is so interesting how this still can be the case, as an aside.

Years ago, I was so blessed to be invited to be a part of a Women's Circle in the centre of Avebury. It was a happy co-incidence, or Divine Timing, of being in the right place at the right time.

I was sat in the pub, in the centre of the Circle, the Red Lion. If you have no idea what or where Avebury is in the world, it is the most amazing Stone Circle, older than Stonehenge in Wiltshire, UK. It is also larger than Stonehenge and has an entire village in the centre of the Stone Circle, two shops, a Post Office, a Pub, houses and all.

Yes really, it is a magical magical, magical place.
Anyways I was sat in the centre of the Circle, in the Pub when a group of friends gathered. They were all locals and lived in or

near the village. I lived an hour's drive away and had happened to be there at that exact time of their gathering. They were just about to go off and make candles for Imbolc. It was a happy co-incidence that I was there, and I was invited along,

And so began the Women's Circle. For several years, at the quarters and cross quarters (Events marked on the Celtic Wheel of the Year) we stopped and honoured, gathered together as a group, and created magical memories together,

After a few of our gatherings we began to get noticed, especially by the men. What were we doing? Were we getting 'too powerful'? Why were we meeting behind closed doors?

The more often we met, the more we were noticed, the more people questioned us.

And so, a group of Women were under suspicion again.

For what was in reality, mainly meeting and chatting over a brew or a glass of wine and putting the world to rights, as men do so often on their boys' nights.

Yes, we created powerful magic together. I really do not want to diminish from that, and it was mainly in the form of Personal Growth. Finding out more about ourselves, becoming more ok with who we are in the world, gaining confidence as we went – because the more we magically learn about ourselves, the more confidence we had.

We gathered, we sang, we danced, we created magic.

And we were under suspicion.

So, once again, Women creating Magic together, even in the 2000's, were under suspicion Whispers were made, rumblings were happening. Men and women alike, were sent to 'talk to us' and find out what we were doing. Looking back with the magic of hindsight, it was truly a harkening back to the dark ages.

And, living through it, being one under suspicion was not fun at all. Especially when no harm was genuinely being done. It was a mad, mad time of heightened emotions all round.

So, with this awareness I have, of what it felt like to be a Woman under suspicion, in the 2000's, I can only imagine how awful it must have been for our Ancestors of Blood and Spirit going back through the generations! I mean!

No wonder they stayed silent!!! No wonder they hid in plain sight! No wonder so much knowledge was lost!

In our Women's Circle, the more suspicious others got, the more we hunkered down and stayed silent, as a form of protection.

In the 2000's.

Now, imagine hundreds and hundreds and hundreds and hundreds and hundreds and hundreds and hundreds of years of Women hunkering down and staying silent all layered up on top of each other.

It is frankly a miracle that we are even having this conversation, you, and I right now. I mean I am SO grateful to the Women who stood up and said NO MORE in our lifetimes, and lifetimes gone by. The fact that I have done so much inner work to even TALK to you about this is a blinking miracle I tell you.

I am not sure if I have mentioned it yet, as a kid, as a teenager, as a young adult I WAS SO SHY. I practiced the art of being seen and not heard. I practiced the art of hiding in plain sight. I practiced the art of simply being present and enjoying the atmosphere of an event without having to engage in conversation with anyone.

Sometimes it is a useful skill to have, and sometimes it has no place.

When it comes to balancing out the Masculine energies of this world with Feminine energies, it is not so useful.

So, here I am the Woman who was known as 'Invisible Kate' in so many circles I had attended, places like Avebury, as for quite a long time, people did not notice me, here I am 'Invisible Kate' writing a book to help Women Shine Their Lights in this world even brighter than they are already.

Nuts huh?

So, yes, it is a miracle that I am writing this book, that you are reading these words, that are filled with heartfelt love for you. I genuinely am so grateful that you, you amazing, incredible, shining being of light, an INCREDIBLE Woman. I am so so so so so so so grateful that you are taking time out of your day to read these words, thank you so so so so so so so much, I truly love you for this, I truly do.

So, circling back, what I am essentially saying is that if I can do this work, if I can shed the layers, one set of shackles after another from the past, if I can release enough shackles and nooses of the past to be sat here at my keyboard even writing these words – YOU CAN TOO, I promise you that.

So, I pose these questions to you: What is holding you back, from taking the steps to shine, that is residual stuff from your past lives? What stuff feels old to you?

It is so hard to relay these words in text form, as in our Shine Your Light Goddess, Shine Your Light Bootcamp we do past life work to uncover these reasons more fully. You might have an inkling of what they are already.

There might be so much goodness here, and you might not have anything. Someone might have already done this work for you in your lineage!

OMG how amazing is that!!! What a gift that someone might have already done the work FOR YOU in your lineage!

That is such an amazing gift!!!!!!

And that is why this work is so, so, so important.

We are not just doing this for ourselves, we are doing this work for the generations of Women to come.

That is how important this work is. It is not just in honour of the amazing Women who stepped before us, our Ancestors of Blood and Spirit, it is not just in pure honour to them, pure gratitude to them.

I mean, think about it, our Ancestors of Blood and Spirit, the Magical ones, the Healers, the Women who had dreams and gifts to share – all those amazing Women and Magicians who stepped before us HAD TO HIDE IN PLAIN SIGHT TO SURVIVE

I mean, sure, they did it for themselves, of course they did If they had not then they would have been burnt at the stake, drowned in the village pond, put in the stocks and had vegetables thrown at them, laughed at, exiled from the village, denounced by family members, you name it, if it was shit it probably would have happened.

Sometimes humans are just horrible right?

And more often, humans are so, so, so lovely.

It is just about surrounding yourself with humans who love you, exactly as you are, because you are amazing exactly as you are. Your 'imperfections' that you are scared of being seen? They are your uniqueness, and this is what the world needs right now.

The world needs YOU.

YOUR skills, your gifts, you!

You are here for a reason, and you have so much to share!

Anyways, I digress...

So, these amazing Ancestors of Blood and Spirit had to hide in plain sight. They had to! Of course, they did it to save their own skin. They also did it for you. They knew that the knowledge they had, the knowledge about that healing flower, that herb, that energy – that Spirit Team, all of that. All of the GOODness in the world HAD to be passed on to new generations. This invaluable knowledge that brings so much GOOD to the world, so much harmony. This knowledge had to be passed on to the generations to come.

And so, they did it for us too, they did it so that we can be here, and we can stand up, we can be SEEN and we can SHARE these gifts with the world.

I mean, imagine a world where all the incredible Lightworkers, Healers, Coaches, where all these amazing Shining Beings of Light step forward and SHINE?

Imagine the balance that this would bring to the male dominated, patriarchal, old boys network world that this would bring, the balance, the harmony, the love,

Imagine the difference that this would make.

Imagine if YOUR descendants of Blood and Spirit (I can't have kids, if you can't too – please don't let it hold you back – you have descendants of Spirit to pass your knowledge onto!)

Imagine if YOUR descendants of Blood and Spirit did not have to do this work? They didn't have to heal the past, to heal the present, to heal the future. Imagine if they just got on with sharing their gifts with the world, without remorse, without fear. Imagine if they did not let anything get in the way, they just, did it?

Wow, what a world that would be!

So, now we are clear that we are not only doing this work to HONOUR and THANK our Ancestors of Blood and Spirit, but we are also doing it for our DESCENDANTS of blood and spirit.

Let us get clear on why we are doing it for ourselves.

Yup, nurturers, I see you, I feel you, those who care so much for others that that is their why.

I see you, I feel you. I mean as a nurturer, I am writing these words down for you. If it was not for you reading this right now, dear reader, then I probably would not have started this work! The inner work and the outer work!

So, I see you, I feel you.

And please know that you are so worth doing this work for, you are so worth it. You can feel so safe to shine and you are allowed to receive the rewards, the abundance, both energetically and financially, you are allowed to receive those rewards.

Place your hands on your heart.

It is safe for me to receive the abundance of the world
It is safe for me to be paid well for what I do
It is safe for me to have a surplus of both financial and emotional energy
It is safe for me to say no to others
It is safe for me to keep reserves in place for me

It is so safe.

Yup, nurturers, I see you, I feel you, I hear you, you are held, you are loved, you are safe, I love you for who you are, right now, reading this book, you are loved.

So, now we have covered the 'Why it is worth us going there' stuff, let's go deeper here.

Have you ever found yourself about to have an uncomfortable conversation with someone, and you have just pulled back from saying the thing that really mattered? That was so important? Have you felt a pull of energy saying 'No, it's not safe to voice your truth?'

Have you ever been about to step on stage to speak, or about to hit publish on a website/course/newsletter, about to sign up to a course, about to take a step towards your goals in life and something stops you, even though you know it is the right thing to do to press send, take that foot on the stage, take that action etc?

Sometimes this fear/protection is real and relevant to this life, and sometimes, yes, we should heed this warning.

And sometimes this fear/protection is real and relevant to past lives. Sometimes it is all about our Ancestors of Blood and Spirit stepping forward to protect us from a perspective of what would have happened if they had done that scary thing.

In their lifetime, if they had done that scary thing, they would have been burnt at the stake, they would have been drowned in the village pond.

They would have been tortured, noses broken, put on the stretching rack, thrown in the tower with the key thrown away. They would have been cast out of their family, their village, their friends, their society.

I mean, the list goes on.

It is, frankly, unsurprising that our Ancestors of Blood and Spirit step forward and try to protect us, it is quite amazing that ANY incredible Women in this lifetime step forward and speak their truth!

The trick is to work out if its past life stuff getting in the way, or present-day stuff getting in the way.

Is it old, old shit, or new shit?

Once we have worked out which it is, we can heed it, honour it, listen to it, and release it if is appropriate to release it.

I mean sometimes it is good to hold onto it.

In the Shine Your Light Goddess, Shine Your Light Bootcamp I show you how to release it. As with all things Spiritual, getting the message across on paper is not always easy, and I will try my best to explain here!

1) Feel into your heart, what is the root of the feeling to stop speaking your truth right now?
2) Is it serving you right now, or is it holding you back?
3) Does it feel right to release it right now?
4) Go into meditation, or write it down and work with a tool that resonates with you, Forgiveness? Tapping? Cord cutting? Releasing of energetic bonds?
5) Sometimes it is all about old promises that have been made. For example, have any of your Ancestors of Blood or Spirit made a vow of silence in their lifetime, that has been passed down the lineage to you? If so, you can renounce any and all vows of silence that have been made in your lineage.
6) THANK your Ancestors of Blood and Spirit, they only did this to PROTECT you, they did these things to HELP you. From the perspective of their lifetime, they made HUGE sacrifices so that YOU could be here, right now, to talk

your talk and bring YOUR magic to this lifetime. Have heartfelt gratitude for those who walked before you and THANK them.

7) Understand that the best way you can thank them is by doing the things that they could not do for fear of recrimination. Speak your truth, make those waves, say you can help people, share your gifts with the world, you have so much to give, you have so many people you can help. You have so much to offer to this generation and those who follow in your footsteps. Speak your truth in honour of those who walked before you.

And breathe, pretty deep right?

Do go for a walk, take a breather after reading this and doing the work. So much happens on an energetic level when we uncover this stuff, and you may feel the world shift a little when you do this work. It is so very powerful, so please be gentle with your energy when you do this work and let it settle before jumping into the next thing on your to do list (again nurturers, I see you).

This work can have a physical effect and well as an energetic effect. You might find that your throat chakra starts releasing and you start coughing. You might find that you are tired emotionally after this, please be gentle with your energy as you do this.

And breathe, you are amazing, you are here for a reason, and you are so loved.

"Take a polaroid picture of where you're going to be in a few years"

Sara Blakely

Chapter 5

I so hope that in reading this book, you are realising just how blinking amazing you are! It is so hard for so many Women to accept that they are incredible. We have been taught from 'little girls' to be in service to those around us.

Receiving compliments is something that was taught to us as being vain, and we should brush off. Please do not brush this one off though. You are so so so so so amazing! You are here for a reason, and you are INCREDIBLE!

Ok, lets continue...-

Let's continue with the Ancestral work. Let's go into the implications of what being silent had on the women who walked before us. What did that mean for them?

- They were silent.

- No-one saw them.

- They did not help people.

- They did not heal as many people as they could have.

- So much powerful healing magic, knowledge and folk lore was lost in the unwritten pages of history.

- They were seen and not heard.

- They were in the shadows.

- They could not voice that they could help others around them.

- They did not share their gifts.

- They could not sell their goods.

- They could not sell their healing herbs.

- They could not sell their wares.

- Just think what the implications of that is and was.

- They could not receive payments in exchange for their knowledge.

- They could not receive the abundance of the world.

- They could not receive wealth.

- They could not be financially independent in most circumstances.

- They were KEPT poor by the men in society.

- They were KEPT poor by the Women in society sometimes.

- They were not allowed to receive wealth.

- They were not allowed to be rich.

- They were encouraged not to SHINE.

- They were encouraged not to be seen.

- They had their independence taken away from them and taught to be reliant on the men around them.

- Sometimes, if they had money, they were asked to give it all away to the Church/Nunnery/Men in their lives!!!! I mean seriously????

- They were the downtrodden Women of the past, BECAUSE they had the KEYS to healing, the KEYS to unlock the poverty, sickness, and depression in their villages.

- They were silenced.

YOU do not have to be.

They were absolutely victims of the time they were born into. YOU do not have to be a victim to it.

How many times have you thought 'Why me?' How many times have you played victim to your surroundings and experiences?

This is where feeling into your own subconscious and daring to explore that maybe, just maybe, it could be that you are connecting to the victim mentality that they, understandably may have been experiencing. If you are reading these words – perhaps you have been guided to release this sense of 'why me' and step forward to Shine? Are these words resonating with you? If so, please read on and explore more with the aid of the workbook.

Is it time to heal, nurture, love and honour them, the victim mentality hangover from their lifetimes, and release that energy with heartfelt love?

Is it time, to coin a phrase, to let it go?

FOR them? So that you can do the work on this earthly plane that they could not do?

Is it time to stand up, speak your truth, speak their truth?

Is it time to receive the abundance and the payments of the world as you serve others and share your gifts?

Is it time to receive the wealth they could not?

In honour of them?

I mean, imagine, if so many amazing Spiritual Women LIKE YOURSELF had a share of the Worlds wealth? I mean, imagine what forces for good can be made there!

Imagine if the worlds wealth had a 50/50 split between Women and Men?

What would the world look like?

What would the world FEEL like?

So, sweet, amazing Goddess, it is so time for you to release these shackles of the past, step forward in this world and SHINE your LIGHT so very brightly!

It is so time. You have SO much to offer, so much to give, so much to share with the world.

You will see in this chapter's section of the workbook there is a sheet with two columns.

On the left-hand side there is space to write down what you would share with the world, if you had no fear of speaking your truth.

What course, sessions, programmes, charity work, conversations in the workplace would you bring to the World.

What conversations would you have? Who would you stand up for? Who would you help?

What would you achieve if you had released the fears around speaking your truth?

Pretty amazing right?

On the right-hand side, the column is what would you receive for speaking your truth? The money to buy a house? The money from a promotion? More time? More energy? More help in what you do? What will you receive?

Do you have any blocks around receiving? Do they need to be healed first? Do you have work to do there?

So many amazing Women do, it is normal, it's part of the process, and its ok. Of course, we go deeper into the healing work on receiving the abundance in Shine Your Light Goddess, Shine Your Light Bootcamp, and for now, go back up to the steps listed above, and do the work from the angle of allowing yourself to receive the abundance of the Universe, and see how it feels.

Again, with this work, you might find yourself tired from the releasing work. I mean we are releasing lifetimes worth of stuff here right; generations of baggage are being let go of, so it's bound to have a physical and emotional effect on you! Be so gentle with you! Be so gentle!

Take time to honour and nurture your soul, your energy, your body through this work. Drink plenty of water and give yourself time after doing each exercise to let the energy settle around you.

And breathe, you are amazing, you are incredible, you are loved, exactly as you are. You are here for a reason.

It is your time to Shine, it is so your time to shine.

Trust me, you would not be reading this book if it wasn't! The Universe has a funny way of working!

"You are never too old to get another goal or to dream a new dream"

C.S. Lewis

Chapter 6

Let us start working within our lifetime now.

Let us now feel the effects of releasing the bonds of the past, so that we can begin to SHINE our light in this lifetime.

It is so, so safe for you to SHINE your Light so brightly, so very safe.

So, now, let's work with the Goddess in the Maiden energy.

So, let's play here, allow your imagination to run wild and be free here.

Allow yourself to play so much here.

Go back to your Maiden Years in this lifetime, grab your workbook, and go back into your memory vaults in this lifetime.

Go back to those late teenage years, your twenties, your thirties those years for you, in this lifetime.

Cast your memory back. Is there anything you would have done differently knowing what you know now?

What advice would you have given the Maiden you, in hindsight?

Having released the shackles of the past, what would you do differently?

Would you have felt safe to Shine? Do you feel safer now to Shine?

Would you be more willing to speak your truth now? Be heard by those who you want to be heard by?

Would you have changed anything?

I know for me, I was far too concerned by what others might think of me, I was too concerned by grades at school, marks given, what my peers thought. Quite frankly, when I went into the workplace I was, in hindsight way too concerned by appraisals, league tables, reports etc. etc. etc.

I wanted to be a 'good girl' and 'conform' somewhere in that. I lost myself, in some ways it was so good to bury myself in my books as a school kid, and by confirming, mainly due to a fear of getting into trouble, I went to an old Grammar school. It had not long been changed from a Grammar school (for those who passed an entrance exam called the 11+ exam) to a secondary school, open to all students of all levels.

It was still run by, frankly, an amazing Woman called Mrs Holland, who wore a Black cap and gown around school and was extremely strict, yet fair, and knew every single schoolgirl's name by sight. It was an all-girls school with one foot firmly in the past and one foot firmly in the future.

On the one hand we were being told to BECOME Lawyers and Doctors, rather than marry them.

On the other hand, we were having typing lessons, so we could get jobs as secretaries and admin assistants in the local firms.

On the one hand we were being taught about the Suffragettes, and our right to vote. We were being taught the power of protest and independent thinking.

On the other hand, I joined secondary school the year they banned Corporal Punishment by Law in the UK. The teachers were finding their way through the transition of being able to rap/whip students as punishment to not being allowed to do so. It was a confusing time for so many. Shouting and detention were commonplace, listening to students, not so much.

So, I really did not want to get into trouble, and I really studied. I worked SO HARD trying to please my family and my teachers, I was that goodie two shoes who immersed herself in the books.

To be fair, I still love learning, I still love studying, I LOVE expanding my mind, and trying new things.

I just do it now because I want to, and I learn about the things that interest me rather than what I am told to study.

I do it now because I love learning new things, not because I am fearful of being shouted at, fearful of being put in detention.

This followed onto to my working life. There were a few glorious years when I joined a large firm locally who employed huge amounts of people in the local area as admin assistants.

For a while there was not much accountability to worry about, you clocked in, did your 8 hours, clocked out again. Every so often we were lucky enough to get a bomb scare (yes really! Lucky!) and we had to evacuate the building and have a few hours off whilst the bomb squad sent the sniffer dogs in to check for bombs.

I know this sounds mad to say lucky, but this was the UK in the 80's, the era of IRA bombings. We lived near to London, on a mainline train route and literally had the Queens back garden stretch to the town we lived in, in the form of Windsor Great Park.

IRA bomb scares, IRA bombs were part of everyday life. We heard about them on the news, we had security training, we noticed that there were no litter bins on the train stations anymore (easy to hide bombs in) and so we just got used to it.

I lived in an apartment block next to the train line for a while. The closest a bomb got to me was when there was a bomb set off on the train line next to my house. I heard the bang, felt the walls shake and went back to sleep as it was the early hours.

These were strange times looking back on things, we just got used to it all and in that window of time, there was very little worry about keeping your job, you just went to work, clocked in, worked, and clocked out.

As a side note, I say lucky to get a bomb scare, to my knowledge we never actually had a bomb. Although who knows if they ever found one and disabled it in their search and sweep of the building. We had to evacuate to the Forbury for a rollcall. The Forbury being Forbury Gardens opposite the office block, however as most of us admin staff were aged 16 – 25, we very often got a roll call check in the Forbury Gardens, and then moved to the other Forbury, a pub, and stayed there all afternoon As a 16-year-old, recovering goodie two shoes, this was far more exciting than working at my desk all afternoon.

Then, as the bomb scares got farther and farther apart, there was more focus on 'can you actually do your job?'

The days of 'a job for life' disappeared and in came 'appraisals' 'time management' sheets 'accountability', even for the managers 'reapplying for your job' as technology advanced and less people were required to do the work.

Rounds and rounds of restructuring came about. Rounds and rounds of redundancies. Reapplying for jobs, followed by more redundancies came about.

And they used those appraisal sheets as weaponry in their arsenal.

So those heady days of just turning up, doing your 8 hours, and going home were gone.

Those days of slacking most of the day, so that you would be offered overtime at time and a half pay were gone.

Basically, appraisals and league tables were back, only this time, the consequences of being low down on the table were not just getting a bad grade, they were getting fired.

Looking back, I am pretty proud of what I did next. Thankfully, we come from a large Irish family and have family all over the World – Australia and New Zealand included. If my father had not decided to say 'fuck it, let's go on holiday' when I was 16, I don't think I would have taken the next steps in life I did.

At 16, as a family, we all took our first plane trip ever to New Zealand to see our family there. Yes, really, the first time I got on a plane, I went to New Zealand, WE went to NZ.

It was definitely a life changing moment. I got to see that there was a life outside of Reading, there were other places to live and work and there was another way of doing things.

So, at aged 19, when the league tables became a weapon of dismissal, I took voluntary redundancy and got on a plane to Australia, alone. The person I was supposed to travel with bailed out a week or two before we were due to go, so, armed with a rucksack I left behind the offices and found myself touring around Australia, one backpacker at a time and seeing the world with very different eyes.

I remember the hardest thing was coming back. I had changed so much, and I had seen things and experienced so many things that my friends here had not.

I had swum with sharks on the Coral Reef. I had travelled down Crocodile infested waters in the Northern Territory. I had climbed Uluru (Ayres Rock), not something I would do now, I hasten to add, it is an Aboriginal Sacred site and is finally respected and honoured as it should be. At the age of 20, in the early 1990's, I did not know any better. I had crossed Sydney Harbour Bridge, I had sat by the Opera House, I had travelled the West Coast and had dolphins swim up to me whilst paddling in the sea. I had crossed the Nullabor plain and seen the seals in Tasmania. I had experienced SO much. I have not even touched on the time I spent in NZ yet, however that was filled with wonderful family memories.

And then I came home, and my friends were still working in the same jobs, going to the same pubs, having the same thing for lunch on the same days.

It was a rude landing.

You would think that I had fully discarded the goodie two shoes mentality huh?

Nope, I went into Sales after a few admin hopping jobs.

Now in Sales, there is a frigging big-league table to get concerned with. How much did you sell this week?

Yup, I went right back into being bogged down in worrying about what others thought of me and I CARED too much. I cared about this more than I cared about my own health, my own mental wellbeing. I worked my arse off to reach targets and was often ignored for doing so.

I mean, I get the idea of motivating staff to do their job and in my experience 'healthy competition' is rarely healthy for all parties involved. Maybe healthy for those in the top third of the chosen league table.

For those in the middle and the bottom of the league table it can be extremely de-motivating and demoralising, which in the case of some companies it is intended to be this way so that those in that part of the league table choose to leave and they can attract different people.

It is not always intended to be that way though, I, as I type these words have literally just resigned from a Business

Networking group, for many reasons. The time, money investment and return just did not stack up for me.

Which, actually, I would have completed my year with the group as it was lovely being part of a group of business owners and feeling as if someone had my back through a pandemic and all.

And

They had a dreaded league table type thing. You were banded in red, amber and green according to how many meetings you had had, how many referrals you had made, and so on and so forth.

For me, my experience was that I began to care TOO much about it. I mean, nothing about the league table was serving my energy, literally nothing, and yet there was my name on it. Week after week I was shown the dreaded table, front and centre of every meeting. Sometimes, I was in the amber, sometimes I was in the red, I never quite made it into the green no matter what I did. I did not have the time or energy in my life to invest into the things the networking group wanted me to do, and that was ok.

And yet, the old me, the Goddess in the Maiden in me began to CARE too much about it, I had to school myself not to care, as when I did, I had a couple of sleepless nights, which quite frankly was ridiculous, utterly ridiculous.

I began to care about what they would think if I left midway through my year.

I began to care WAY too much about what the group thought about me.

So, the Goddess in the Maiden that cared was carrying that energy forwards.

Even though it was draining me energetically.

Even though it was not serving my business. Very few of the other members of the group even understood what I did, let alone referred anyone to me!

Even though it was costing me valuable time in my business, it was easily taking up a day a week of my time meaning I was not connecting with clients in that time. I was not fixing broken links on my website in that time. I was not joining networking groups where they DID understand my business.

And yet I kept attending, I kept going, for fear of what they would think of me!

Once I tuned into walking my talk, tuned into thinking what advice I would give to the Goddess in the Maiden energy who cared, more importantly, can you imagine what the Goddess in the Crone from any previous lifetime would say about that??

I can hear the swearing from here!!! So much giggling and wry laughter!!!

I can literally HEAR the 'Fuck that shit, fuck what they think, do what's right for you and leave already. Who CARES what they think!!!!'

So, 3 days ago I resigned, 9 months into my years commitment (something the old me would never have done!!! I was that 'goody-two-shoes!!'

Hmmm, wonder where that name came from? I am going to have to do some research on that!

Anyways, I digress! I was that goody two shoes, and I released it, reflected on what would serve me the most, what would serve my business, my clients, my mental health, my energy.

And I resigned. Oh my, it feels so freeing, so wonderful AND I am noticing SO MANY holes in my business that were created in the last 9 months whilst I paid too much attention to the networking business, rather than my business!

So, this is a real-life example of how looking at how I could break the shackles of the present, to SHINE more brightly in this world. Tuning into the Goddess in the Maiden energy and listening to the advice that I would give her and listening to where it was clunking on things in my present. In my current reality. How I created REAL LIFE changes in my life right now.

And it feels bloody good. I am probably hiding a little right now from how good it feels because I am still a little stunned by how good it feels!!!!

And breathe!!!!!!

So, enough about me, what advice would you give the Goddess in Your Maiden? What advice would you give? Do you need to hear it in your present right now and is it an ironic plot twist that actually the Goddess in the Maiden is giving you advice too?

And breathe! A lot to take in that!

And breathe.

Another very powerful exercise to do here is to go over your memory vaults and see if you stayed silent in times where you now wish that you had shouted your truth from the rooftops?

Did you stay silent for other people's feelings? Did you stay silent for fear of ruffling others feathers?

Do you regret staying silent?

Three things you can do here:

1) Write all these things down, say them out loud and burn that piece of paper.

2) Go back in time in meditation and forgive the you that made the decision to stay silent. You were so young and did what you thought to be right at the time. Forgive the you that decided to stay quiet, and perhaps forgive anyone you spoke your truth too and they told you to stay quiet – it does not make it right that this happened. However, those energy hooks are not serving you now and sometimes it's just a whole lot easier to release that shit and move on with your life.

3) Of course, you can always speak your truth now. Ruffle those feathers now, especially if it will protect future generations!!!

A lot to be said about the Goddess in the Maiden, right?

This can be really powerful work, it can be so healing, it can be so emotional, so as always, please do be so gentle with your energy and allow space for the memories and the healing to flow, be so kind to you.

If it brings up things that It would be useful to see a therapist about, do so! Please value yourself and do so!!!

Of course, we have more support in the Shine Your Light Goddess, Shine Your Light Bootcamp, of course we do! So, if it speaks to you, come join us!

With such a huge hug of love! From my heart to yours, huge hugs!

"Sometimes you will never know the value of a moment, until it becomes a memory!

Dr. Seuss

Chapter 7

Goddess in the Mother.

This is a hard one for some to even begin reading. If you, like me, can't have children, you may feel like skipping this chapter.

If you feel so much pain to even read the words 'Mother' please feel free to skip this chapter and revisit it at a later date. You do not need to brace yourself and do it anyway, be kind to you, nurture your soul and just skip this chapter. I know for a while, whilst I was still accepting that I can't have children in this lifetime, just the word 'Mother' would trigger me, so I understand totally and you do not have to keep reading just because, you really don't.

And please know that this chapter is written with heartfelt compassion from someone who understands how it feels to try for a baby. I tried for 10 years with my ex. The pain was so hard to process, and writing these words brings so much rawness back. I understand, it took me YEARS of inner work to even begin to heal from the pain of not being able to give birth to physical children in this lifetime. If it is still too raw for you, please skip over and come back to this chapter.

What I began to learn after beginning the healing process around this, is that Goddess in the Mother is not just about giving birth to children. That took time to hear, even longer to feel, and once that knowledge landed in my being, I began to be able to understand my Goddess in the Mother period in my life and truly honour it. I began to be able to feel like a Mother of the Creation of the way I live my life.

That took so much time. If you are reading these words nodding along, I am sending you so much love, so much love, from my heart to yours, so much love, so many hugs, so much love.

And how does the Goddess in the Mother period of our lifetime work?

The Goddess in the Mother phase is about CREATION.

The Goddess in the Mother phase is about giving birth to IDEAS.

The Goddess in the Mother phase is about giving birth to BUSINESSES.

The Goddess in the Mother phase is about NURTURING OUR SOULS.

The Goddess in the Mother phase is about PASSING ON our knowledge to others. Whether physical children or students of our courses, our programmes, our Spiritual Lineages. It's about passing on our knowledge to our descendants of Spirit.

And of course, The Goddess in the Mother period in our lifetimes is about giving birth to physical, beautiful babies in this lifetime. If you are so blessed to have children, give them an extra squeeze tonight!

So, what I am saying is please skip this chapter if it is too raw, and please read knowing that it is written with heartfelt compassion.

So, so often when Mothers give birth, all the energy is put, understandably, into their baby. All of the mother's energy is put into the baby, loving the baby, feeding the baby, nurturing the baby, looking after the baby 24/7.

Whether it be a physical baby, or an energetic baby as listed above.

Then, the baby grows up, and gets his/her own life and goes into their own life, even businesses can do that.

How many times have you heard that the business has run away with itself, become out of hand?

So often the Mothers are forgotten about!

So often the Mothers forget who they are!

So often the Mothers lose themselves in all of this, so often

In the times gone by, so many of the Mothers were revered by so many cultures. The Mothers were honoured and respected as much as the children.

In times gone by, before the shift to the Patriarchal Society we find ourselves in today, Women were HONOURED.

In cave paintings, there are so many amazing Images of Women, of the Divine Feminine, of the Goddess, Women were so honoured and respected.

And then the balance shifted.

God became a single parent.

Men began running the Temples, the Churches, Men decided to shift the balance.

And the balance shifted.

I am so looking forward to the time that equanimity returns, and there is an even balance between Men & Women, Women & Men. I see younger generations and I hope it is closer than it appears.

There is definitely a shift happening, there is definitely a shift.

In times gone by, surnames were passed down via the Mothers Line, rather than the Fathers line. It shifted. It will be interesting to see if that shifts again as time flows on.

I used to see it as written in stone that the name is passed on via the Fathers line. Such a male energy that.

It reminds me of the difference that is apparent in the way the men I see in business networking, approach their businesses, versus Women.

Men 'crush' their goals.
Men 'hunt' down customers.
Men 'conquer' a market.

Women 'nurture' their business relationships.
Women 'tend' to their customers' needs.
Women 'join in' a conversation in their market, bringing their gifts to the table.

This, please understand me, is not a 'Man bashing' exercise. I truly, truly believe in the power of balance, and the two energies fusing together can be off the charts incredible.

And this is about honouring the Divine Feminine, in this lifetime.

The Goddess in YOU.

The Goddess in YOUR Mother stage of your life.

If the Goddess in YOU allows herself to be seen, allows the shackles of the past to be released, then what can you achieve?

What balance can YOU bring to this Global conversation?

What balance can you bring to the world?

The possibilities are blinking amazing!!!!

So, thoughts to ponder on here.

What is it you want to give birth to in this lifetime?

What legacy do you want to leave in this world? However big or small? You will leave an imprint on this world, big or small. So, do you want to intentionally leave a legacy that is thought through?

What, do YOU want to nurture?

What dreams do YOU want to bring into creation? Into a physical reality?

Are you reading this, thinking 'I have already created them, next!'? Then my question is, do you want these gifts to be passed on to generations to come, or to die with you when the time comes? Either is absolutely fine, of course, it's just about mindfully making that decision and planning accordingly.

It's about deciding whether your creations of spirit become 'You and Daughters' or simply 'You in this lifetime'.

Once you have decided, then plans can be made accordingly and mindfully. Blinking amazing that!

So, now you have thought about this a little deeper; consider what has been stopping you take the steps you want to take to achieve these dreams, wishes and goals, to give birth to your creations.

Are you scared of being seen?

Are you scared of being honoured too much?

Are you scared of being out on a pedestal and become ostracised from society?

Are you scared of out earning the men in your life?

Are you scared of becoming RICHER than the men in your life?

Are you scared of upsetting the equilibrium in your life?

Are scared people will laugh at you?

Are you scared people will be-little your ideas?

Are you scared?

I know I was! I know I have done SO MUCH inner work on all of the above, especially when it came to out earning my Father!!!

Pretty ridiculous right, when you think on it. If a son out earned their Father, it is seen as successful, if a Daughter out earns her Father, it can be seen as emasculating and embarrassing her whole family!!!! Nuts!!!!

When I first earnt my first paycheque, my Father looked at my paycheque and exclaimed 'oh look! I pay more tax than you earnt this month!!!' On reflection, I now realise that my Father absolutely was dealing with his own money blocks at the time, and the intention was absolutely not to crush my excitement at bringing home my first full time works paycheque. Those words are still words I am working on, and I wonder now how much I have kept myself small so as not to earn more than him as the years went on!

So, what are the 'negative' consequences of you Shining Your Light even more brightly in this world? What are reasons that have been holding you back? What is it that has really been stopping you taking these actions?

What can you release around that? What can you forgive? What shifts can you make?

What inner work can you do to heal from this? What inner work can you release?

It really does create shifts, ripples in the Universe.

A butterfly flaps their wings in one corner of the World causes a tsunami in another right?

Once you release these fears and worries, what are you going to give birth to? What creations are you going to bring into the world, with or without judgement?

What are you going to give birth too?

Feel the excitement and the love for your creation that you are about to give birth too!

Feel it, really feel it!

So often we do not allow ourselves the time to feel the excitement of the creation and planning stages. We don't allow ourselves the feeling of excitement as we bring about creations into this world. When a baby is in the womb, we have 9 months to tend and nurture and fall in love with our babies.

So often we do not allow ourselves the time to love the process of CREATION in our lives, our businesses, our everything. So, I invite you to really enjoy and fall in love with your creation.

And please remember, these creations are to be birthed into the world! They are to be released and allow the world to love them too. Scary huh!

And breathe – you have totally got this!

So, in our Shine Your Light Goddess, Shine Your Light Bootcamp Community, it is worth saying that so many Shining Goddesses who have gone through the modules have found themselves doing some major healing work around their relationship with their Mothers here.

You may feel called to call your Mother and just reconnect, you may not.

Your Mother may have passed over, and if so, I am sending you a hug. You might want to light a candle and just open the space up to remember all that was wonderful about your relationship with your Mother, you might not.

You may want to take time to consider how your Mother may have hid her light in this world. How did she not Shine? Where did she dim her light in order to make peace with her role as Mother in the family?

I know that my Mother avoided political debates so often, as my Father had some different views to my Mother. I remember asking my Mother what she thought, and she would avoid answering 'so as not to make waves Kate'. It is only in adulthood that I have realised just how much my Mother stayed silent in conversations we had around the kitchen table.

On reflection, where and how did your Mother stay silent, hide her light? Can you connect with your Mother now and ask her about it? Can you listen now? Or is it not appropriate given the family dynamics?
Just reflecting on this may just be another unlocking in releasing the shackles of the past

And breathe, you have got this.

Emotional as it is, you have totally got this.

And breathe.

It is ok for you to release these shackles. It is ok for you to release these shackles and Shine Your Light so brightly. It is so safe for you to SHINE your LIGHT in this world, it is so safe!

And breathe. You are here for a reason, you are loved, you are so safe. It is so safe for you to SHINE, the time is now, and you are so SAFE to SHINE.

And breathe, you have totally got this!

With SO MUCH GRATIUDE to the MOTHERS who WALKED before us, Thank you so much, thank you indeed xxx

With so much Gratitude indeed.

Please remember, you are so welcome to join us in circle in our Shine Your Light Goddess, Shine Your Light Bootcamp, just head here to join

https://my-natural-happiness.newzenler.com/courses/shine-your-light-goddess-shine-your-light
QR code for course enrolment

More healing to be done around that, I am sure!

"Make yourself a priority, at the end of the day, you are your longest commitment!

Anon

Chapter 8

Goddess in the Crone work

When we are the Maiden stage of life, or the Maiden stage of a project, we think we know it all! That gives us amazing confidence and excitement to start and keep going. I mean, we have all the answers, right?!!

When we are in the Mother stage of life, or a project we are a little scared however know there is no option but to birth our babies, our projects into the world.

And, when we are in the Crone stage of life, or a project, we have learnt stuff.

We have seen patterns emerge, we have seen and learnt things and we have the benefit of experience, we may look back on things we have done in the past with the benefit of hindsight and wonder if we would have done things differently perhaps. The challenge sometimes can be to look back with hindsight at situations we were in, advice we may have listened to that was great. Advice that was not great and see our part in it.

Knowing that we did the best we could with the knowledge we had at the time is huge, knowing that we did what we could and the best we could do.

So, the challenge can be, not being a bitter old crone! Sometimes, just sometimes if we allow the bitter old crone time out to play, that can be a healing and cathartic experience on its own. So, as always, balance is the key here.

(Side note: when I used to hear people say things like 'This info will give you the keys to be healed' I used to think I would be given a literal key! Linear brain here!)

This chapter is about learning about the Crones in our lineage. The Crones in our family. The Crones in the direction we are moving in our lives.

This chapter is about being humble enough to learn from them (I mean, the Maiden knows it all right!!! This can be a challenge!!!!)

This chapter is about learning from the Crones in our arena and hearing the wisdom of their experience.

Hearing it and deciding for yourself what information is relevant in this stage of your life, and what information is outdated and can be released into the history books.

This is about reminding you that you can listen to their experience and feel what resonates and what doesn't.

This is about listening to the part of the Crone that has pure wisdom for you.

So, what can you learn from the Crones in your world, so that you can shine from within and enjoy life, and bring magic in?

Sometimes it takes so much to listen to others and hear their advice, especially if it goes against what you want to hear!

In your workbook you will see that there is a whole section dedicated to learning from others

With what you are birthing at the moment, who are the experts in that field?

What can you learn from them?

What can you listen to?

What, would you do differently?

(You don't have to follow everything they say, if it does not resonate with you DON'T do it!!!!)

Example for me, my first business coach told me I had to join a particular networking group to springboard my coaching success. I ignored it for years as it wasn't resonating AT ALL with me. Finally, a local group of this particular networking group, at a time and day I could do, I joined it. I met lovely people and made some good connections. Ultimately though it drained me, as the group did not suit my energy at all!

The benefit of this hindsight after years of wondering, 'should I just join or not?', is that listening to my gut instinct in the first place would have saved me a ton of time and money!

So, listen and absorb yourself in those who are experts in the field you are birthing a conversation into. Listen, see what resonates, what doesn't and hear what people are saying!

Know that what you bring to the subject, to the conversation is unique. You are you, you are unique, and people will listen to you BECAUSE you are you, and your energy resonates with them.

So, learn, absorb, listen, and hear the Crones, the experts in your field advice. Listen to the Women, the Elders, the Crones that have walked before you, they will have valuable advice to hear.

Please remember in some fields YOU ARE THE CRONE, and you can share so much with others in that field.

Consider what these are and feel into them. Please remember that you can help so many people by sharing your wisdom with them. Think of the time you can save someone if you just share your wisdom with them! What would it have been like if someone had done that for you?

And breathe, a lot to process right!

Whilst we are in the Crone Chapter, how about you go and have a chat with the Crones in your family? If they are still with you on this earthy plain you are so blessed!

Ask them about their Maidenhood! What did they get up to in their youth? When a Woman is in her Crone stage, she is far more likely to share the naughty stuff if asked!

I did this with my Nan just before she died. The stories she told me about what they got up in between the bombs landing in London would make your hair curl!!! (Nan was a Londoner and lived through the blitz, they truly lived life on the edge!)

Goddess is in the Crone!

In Shine Your Light Goddess Bootcamp we go back into the mists of time and learn from the Crones in our lineage, those who walked before us. We go back into the past and learn from them, to land into the present with the benefit of their knowledge and take our steps into the future with the benefit of hindsight. It is really hard to take you through that journey through the medium of paper, so for that one, you will have to join us in circle to experience this I'm afraid!

Here is the link to find out more about our Shine Your Light Goddess, Shine Your Light Bootcamp

https://my-natural-happiness.newzenler.com/courses/shine-your-light-goddess-shine-your-light

QR code for course enrolment

You will find the info on my website too
www.mynaturalhappiness.com

QR code for website

Learn, listen, hear, and know that you have the benefit of hindsight now. Have a look at the notes you made in the last chapter and over in the workbook around what you would birth and look, feel. Is there anything you would do differently with the benefit of hindsight that the Goddess in the Crone gifted to you?

Perhaps you will take more action and stop procrastinating, as life is too short, just perhaps?

Saying this as much to me as to you right now!!!

And breathe. Take a drink of water, go for a walk and feel into the knowledge that has been imparted to you. Allow it to settle into you before you move on to the next chapter. I know you are hungry for knowledge and allow it to settle into you before you move on.

And breathe – you have got this!

You are amazing, it is your time to Shine, and the time is now

"Sit with the winners, the conversation is different"

Anon

Chapter 9

Have a check in, see how you are feeling? Right now? Are you feeling nervous? Excited? Happy? A little sad? Excited to work with the Universe and SHINE your LIGHT so brightly?

You might be feeling a little nervous about taking those steps to SHINE your light so brightly and see what is on the other side.

Breathe, you have totally got this.

I hear you; I see you and I feel you; it is ok. As I type these words, I realise I am a little nervous about writing the chapter as the more I write, the closer I will be to having this book finished, published and in your hands.

The fact you are reading these words right now means so much to me, thank you, thank you so much. Part of me is excited that you are reading this, part of me is scared of that. The fact I am nervous about completing this chapter means I understand that you might be nervous about the steps that you have decided to take and Shine your Light so brightly.

Take a moment to think about the people who you will help by taking these steps.

Think about the shifts you can help them make.

Think about what you can bring to the table.

Think about someone hearing your message, your story, your words, and the difference that will make to the world.

Breathe that in, I know it feels a little scary and you, have totally got this (I am saying this as much to myself as to you!)

Right let's get started. Breathe. You have totally got this!

So, this Chapter is about dreaming big and Shining your light so brightly.

Sometimes when we step up to Shine, some blocks may arise as you do this.

You might find that as you step up to Shine, you release so much fear around speaking your truth in a kind, compassionate way. If you have stayed silent until almost breaking point in certain arenas in your life, and you begin to speak your truth there, others may not like it.

Please remember that is their stuff, not yours. I have no doubt that you will speak your truth in a kind, compassionate manner and if it holds a mirror up to those around you to see their reflection in this lifetime, that is their stuff not yours.

Sometimes it is about boundaries and recognising that sometimes saying yes to yourself means saying no to others as you walk through this lifetime.

For example, as I was recording the module for this section of this bootcamp, I found myself voicing my thoughts more and more in various online forums standing up for kindness as opposed to the anger, which upset people so much.

Another thing that happened was, as a kid I was bullied awfully, especially by one particular family. As an adult I can have compassion for the bullies as I dread to think what their home life was like for all 3 of the children in the family, to become horrific bullies. I have done so much releasing work around that over the years that I can't begin to tell you.

Anyways, as I was recording the module for this chapter, having not seen or heard anything from that family since I left school, Facebook has been kind to me! The day I recorded this module, back in summer 2020, in a pandemic, a member of that family commented on a post I placed on a forum. I knew I had to do more clearing work and more forgiving work in that moment, as oh boy! What a mix of emotions that was!

I can't imagine how tough it must be if you were the bully in school, so I have pure compassion for that.

As I raised my vibration doing the work, more stuff appeared to clear.

So, please know, if more things crop up as you do the work in these pages, please know, it is just about clearing more stuff so that you can shine your light so much brighter in this world.

I see it as an onion with a diamond in the centre. The more layers you uncover and clear, the more layers you see.

Know that it is part of the process and is the work. Be kind to yourself and compassionate indeed.

Shining your Light and spreading kindness does not mean you have to be a pushover. So often it is about bringing in strong boundaries as you Shine brighter so that you can maintain your energy levels as you go.

Work with what works for you, is it forgiveness work? Cord Cutting? (You will find a free cord cutting mediation in the bonus resources of your book).

Please know, you don't have to do it all at once. Incremental upgrades can be so much more sustaining in the long run. So, please do not think that you have to clear all the blocks in one hit, by any means, one layer, one step, one block released at a time is so so so so powerful. So, please, please, go at your own energy pace here.

As we move deeper into this work, let us look at where we are going next in our lives with this work.

What do you want to achieve in this world with this lifetimes worth of wisdom you have received?

Now is the time we Shine Our Lights in this world and be counted for! Now is the time we bring even more balance to the world.

We are standing on the shoulders of giants.

We are standing on the shoulders of the Women who walked before us, who fought for us to have a vote, fought for us to have a voice, fought for our rights in employment fought for our rights as human beings.

Fought for equality to be shown in tv programmes For Women who said, 'that is not ok!' We are standing on their shoulders so that our descendants of blood and spirit have less to fight for and can achieve even more than we dream possible.

Popping in here that I have been watching re-runs of 'Only Fools and Horses' a UK Comedy show of old. I have watched it for years and loved it. I still love it as the comedy aspect is so good, and the more I watch the show having been called to write this book, the more I realise how badly Women were represented in it! Del, the main character, certainly did not speak well about Women, especially those Rodney was looking to date. I have never noticed it before I was called to write this book.

So, we are standing on the shoulders of those who DID notice it and CALLED it out.

It is so interesting how when I was emerging out into the clubbing scene, Women who went out and just 'lived life large' were demonised by the British Press. The men who did the same were applauded!!!!

So, thank you to the likes of Zoe Ball, Sara Cox and the other 'IT' girls of the clubbing scene, you paved the way for us to be free. Thank you!

'The gang of Ladettes including Sara Cox and Zoe Ball rule the 1990s party scene, dancing on the tables and drinking men under them'

The phrase 'ladette' was coined by FHM in 1994

So, my question is how are you going to stand up and be counted in this lifetime? Both for yourself and those to come? What shifts are you going to ripple out to the world?

They can be small, or large. The butterfly causing a tsunami.

They can be calling out misinformation where you see it or running for the Presidency of the United States.

What shifts are you going to bring to the World as you Shine Your Light so much brighter?

What magic are you bringing to this lifetime?

You are reading this book for a reason, what is that reason?

If not now when? Put a date in the diary to take action, for all of those who walked before you and ahead of you.

Dream big here. No one has to know your answers. You do not have to show your answers to anyone, so start writing down your answers and then you can plot a course to get there.

It all starts with putting a marker down in the sands of time.

Then you can begin to make your way there, in this lifetime.

Feel into this, where do want to be with this work. Dream big and work backwards.

You have totally got this and breathe.

You are here for a reason, you have been born in this time, for a reason. You are an amazing Shining being of Light and you are here for a reason. It is so safe for you to Shine, and you have totally got this.

With such a huge, huge hug of love,

From my heart to yours, you have totally got this!

Tune into the future you that has taken action on her dreams, actions on her wishes, learning from the past to create magic in her future. Tune into the future you who has achieved what you seek.

Listen and learn from her. Tune into her, listen and learn from her.

What lessons does she have for you?

Did she care about getting that email out on time for work? Or did she care more about getting home on time for her family?

What lessons does she have?

Listen, learn. Hear her story and tune into her footsteps. Let the magic unfold from there.

Feel her energy. Feel her gratitude she has that you took those first steps in this time.

Feel her inspire you with the fact that the work you are doing now makes a difference.

Feel her love for you embrace you.

Listen to her words, listen to her advice on what to do next, listen.

Feel her embrace you with gratitude.

Feel her. Feel the Woman you are stepping into, the Goddess you are stepping into.

Know that it is completely possible for you to step into your dreams, completely possible.

I remember doing this exercise when I was in the Corporate World. I always knew that I wanted to be self-employed. I always knew that this was my dream, and I did this exercise, stayed focused on my dream and allowed the magic to unfurl.

Of course, there is a mundane reason for this too. When you are clear on the direction you want to walk in this life, when you are clear about the path you are on, you can take mindful steps to get there.

You make decisions in alignment with your path.

For example, with my goal of going self-employed: -

I spent those 30 minutes on my website after work a few days a week.

I created a Facebook page.

I told people about my dream.

I ran weekend retreats.

I attended courses on Reiki, Mindfulness, Meditation.

I invested in business courses designed for Spiritual Women.

I decided on an amount of time that I could realistically dedicate to building my business whilst still employed and stuck to it.

So yes, I weaved in magic to the mundane. By magically tuning into the future, I wanted to create for myself, I could tune into the potential

I tuned in to the love and the excitement for achieving my dream.

I visualised myself where I am now, sat typing these words, writing this book. In my pj's with a mug of tea in hand, with no-one telling me what to do, what do wear, how to act. No-one telling me I should meet their standards which are not aligned to mine in any way. (I would rather get something done in my pj's than put pressure on myself to get dressed first, and not do it at all. Just this thought alone would horrify some of my former bosses!!!!)

I visualised all of this, which then meant that I got excited for that future and took practical steps to align myself to this destiny, which had a compounding effect and here I am, typing away on my laptop in my jim jams before I serve some amazing clients later on today.

So good, this shit works, it really does!

Enjoy, have fun with this. Dance in your lounge, get excited and enjoy this energy SO MUCH.

Shine Your Light on the path you are looking to walk along and enjoy!
Start of module 7 now …. Getting there, this book is a being written!!!

And breathe indeed!

"Why fit in when you were born to stand out?"

Dr. Seuss

Chapter 10

You may notice shifts in your energy, just by reading this book, even if you have not done any of the exercises listed within. You may notice shifts in your energy and this may be unsettling if this is new for you.

Just be gentle with you and allow the energy to settle. There is a path to walk, and we do not need to run. Just by taking small steps every day towards our goals can create massive results.

Incremental steps often create stronger foundations than giant leaps.

One step, however small they are, can create massive results!

And taking those steps where I feel resistance are so magical!!!

Standing up for what I believe in is amazing!

Being WHO I AM in full colour, in my pj's is so so so so so so so so so good!!!

I promise you, being who you really are is so much less exhausting than trying to live life with a 'face on'.

When you step forward and SHINE YOUR LIGHT so brightly, shining who you are from within is ENERGISING.

The more you do this work, the more you help the balance in the world.

The microcosm affecting the macrocosm affecting the microcosm.

So, enjoy SHINING Your Light so beautifully.

So, next steps? Integration?

Of course, you can come join our Shine Your Light Goddess, Shine Your Light Bootcamp.

Here is the link again - https://my-natural-happiness.newzenler.com/courses/shine-your-light-goddess-shine-your-light

QR code for course enrolment

It will be so wonderful to see you there if it is speaking to you.

And, if you are not resonating with that right now, have some clear thoughts on how you are going to Shine Your Light so brightly in this world.

Put notes in your diary to revisit your goals.

Put notes in your diary on the steps you are going to take to get to your goal.

Buy an anchor, such as jewellery, a keyring or an object that reminds you of your dreams. Anchor your learnings and dreams in there so that every time you feel like retreating into your fears, you can look at this anchor which reminds you to take steps towards your goal

I made myself some soap and so, every time I wash my hands, I say to myself 'It's safe for me to Shine, its safe for me to achieve my goals'

It is a wonderful reminder!

Ongoing support is so available; we have the Seeds of Change Programme, Shine Your Light Goddess, Shine Your Light Bootcamp, so many wonderful resources. If you are looking for ongoing support, just reach out!

I can't wait to see you Shine! Post a pic of your anchor on Instagram tagging me @kate_the_happiness_fairy with the #shineyourlightgoddess as I would love to see them!

With such a huge hug,

Kate xxx

"Be who you are and say what your feel, because those who mind don't matter, and those who matter don't mind"

Dr. Seuss

Resources

Purchase my cards –

https://my-natural-happiness.newzenler.com/f/oracle-cards
QR code for Oracle Cards

Workbook: https://my-natural-happiness.newzenler.com/f/shine-your-light-goddess-shine-your-light-the-workbook
QR code for workbook

Link to the Shine Your Light Goddess, Shine Your Light Bootcamp.
https://my-natural-happiness.newzenler.com/courses/shine-your-light-goddess-shine-your-light
QR code for course enrolment

Find out more about Kate at www.mynaturalhappiness.com
QR code for website:

And www.magicalcourses.mynaturalhappiness.com
QR code for more courses

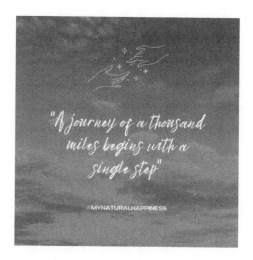

"A journey of a thousand miles begins with a single step"

#MYNATURALHAPPINESS

In the Seeds of Change Programme, and Shine Your Light Goddess, Shine Your Light Bootcamp spaces we talk a lot about aligning our actions with our dreams,

So, my question for you is what action can you take today that is in alignment with your dreams?

What one thing can you do today, that is in alignment with your big goal?

Sending a huge hug for your day,

With so much love,
Kate xxx

All you need is love.
But a little chocolate
now and then
doesn't hurt.

CHARLES M. SCHULZ

Ah, all you need is love in this world.

This is so true!

I mean, imagine if you loved yourself as unconditionally as you do your favourite bar of chocolate (or insert your passion food name right here).

Imagine if you accepted yourself as unconditionally as your favourite chocolate bar?

Imperfections, knocks and all?

Imagine if you loved, and accepted yourself, exactly as you are right now, as much as you loved and accepted your favourite chocolate bar (or insert name of your passion food right here)

Wrapper and all?

Imagine what that would feel like?

Imagine how you would walk through this world?

Imagine, just imagine what you would achieve!

So much of what we do in both the Seeds of Change Programme, and Shine Your Light Goddess, Shine Your Light Bootcamp is around loving, and accepting yourself exactly as you are, scrunchy wrapper and all, so that you can achieve your dreams, wishes and goals so much quicker.

So, love is all you need, self-love and self-acceptance is even better.

And chocolate is sooooo good too!

Have a fabulous day!

With love,
Kate xxx

BEING IN THE MOMENT
JUST BREATHE
IN THE MOMENT RIGHT
NOW

Sometimes it is good to stop and breathe and feel. I invite you to take a moment to just take a deep breath and check in with how you are feeling right now.

How are you? How are you feeling within? How are you?

Place your hand on your heart and feel into the answers, releasing any judgements around it, any fears, any guilts around how you are feeling and just feel into it - creating an awareness around how you really feel.

And breathe. Just be totally ok with where you are at. It is what it is, and you are amazing exactly as you are.

And breathe, you are amazing.

It is good to stop and just enjoy the moment along the way. This can be hard to do sometimes, especially if you have work stuff, family politics or tough decisions to make in your life at the moment. Those thoughts can creep in anywhere and everywhere.

And enjoying being in the moment can provide so much stress release. If you are watching a tv show, being in the moment and watching the tv show, if you are at the beach, being in the moment and focusing on the beach sounds and smells, even for a minute, can make a huge difference to our stress levels.

I am taking a moment of pause, to lovingly challenge you to being in the moment for one whole minute at some point this week. Fully focusing on what you are doing, for one whole minute, and enjoy it!

And breathe!

If you want more mindfulness tips, and to learn how to weave so many amazing mindfulness tools and techniques into your daily life, then do have a nose at my 8 Weeks of Mindfulness Course below. You could be enjoying your first module within minutes.

As always, if you want more info on joining our Seeds of Change Community, or our Shine Your Light Goddess, Shine Your Light Community, just drop me a message and let's talk,

https://my-natural-happiness.newzenler.com/courses/8-weeks-of-mindfulness

QR Code for mindfulness

With such a huge hug of love, from my heart to yours, Kate xxx

Most mornings I head outside for a few minutes of calm and meditation before I start my day.

Some days are 'meh' some days are magical, and it is a beautiful way to start the day.

Some days, I am shown wonderful messages in nature by Spirit, for example this beautiful leaf, filled with water on the ground.

What is beautiful about a dead leaf I hear you ask?

Well, if the tree had not decided to release the leaf, the tree would be struggling to keep this leaf, and all the other leaves alive. By releasing this leaf, the tree can focus its energy on feeding, nurturing and nourishing the leaves it chose to keep.

And by discarding this leaf, it has found a new purpose, it has become a water bowl for the bees, the insects, the birds. This leaf now has a new purpose on this earth!

A win all round indeed!

So, my message I received on the morning I took this picture was 'What can I release in my life now, so I may better serve that I choose to keep'

Pretty profound right?

Thank you leaf! Thank you, Spirit!

So, what can you release in your life so you have more energy for what you keep?

We talk ALOT about releasing the shackles of the past, so we can step into our future so much lighter in both our Shine Your Light Goddess, Shine Your Light Bootcamp and our Seeds of Change Programme.

With such a huge hug of love,
Kate xxx

At the end of the last chapter, I posed the question 'what would you like to release over the next few weeks, so you have more energy for what you want to keep?'

I thought I would share something that formed during lockdown, that I definitely want to keep!

Some mornings, if it is beautiful and I am awake early enough, I will make a brew and head out into the fields behind my house IN MY PJ'S!

Now, pre lockdown, I would never have dreamt of going for a walk in my pj's with a brew near my house, I mean I have done this in Avebury many times, Glastonbury too, however near my house?
Where people might see me? No way!

Lockdown brought with it a sense of 'frankly I could not give a shit what people think' and off I go, brew in hand.

Funny thing is, I have got out for an early morning walk WAY MORE than I ever did, as now all it takes is throw a tea bag in a mug with some milk, bung a coat on and off I go.

It is SO much less hassle, so much quicker and I don't take up precious thinking time. I just do it. I rarely bump into anyone as it is early doors.

Imperfect action beats perfect inaction every single day of the week.

What can you do imperfectly today to just get something done? I would love to hear!

With so much love,
Kate
xxx

We talk a lot about this on the Seeds of Change Programme, if you want more info, just dm me!

A loving reminder to you as you Shine Your Light so brightly in this world.

Each time you say yes to others, please make sure you're not saying no to yourself #boundaries

Giving yourself permission to say no to others requests on your time is one of the biggest acts of self-care you can give yourself.

We even dedicate AN ENTIRE MODULE of the Seeds of Change Programme to creating healthy boundaries, it is that important.

So, next time someone asks if you can quickly do this, or volunteer to do that, please feel into your heart, releasing any guilt around saying the word no, and decide if YOU want to say yes, or no.

Then just reply, yes, or no. You do not even have to give a reason if it's a no!

Top tip here: - if you say no, follow it up with a question, for example, "no, I'm afraid I can't help you there have you seen the weather report for this weekend? It looks dreadful! I am thinking of heading to the cinema and staying dry!"

Try it and see how empowering it feels!

With so much love,
Kate xxx

p.s. If you want to find out more about our Seeds of Change Programme, just drop me a message and let's talk!

About the Author

Kate worked in the Corporate environment for more years than she can remember, working 80 plus hours a week, on the Hamster Wheel and working hard to achieve other people's dreams.

Kate was stressed, rundown and always knew that there was something more in life for her – there was always an inner knowing that she was meant to serve others in a deeper, more Spiritual Way, and yet she continued on the thread of the Corporate World as it felt safe.

A defining moment in Kate's life was in September 2009 when she had a fairly major car accident, driving along the M4 in Berkshire, she fainted and woke up in a ditch – Kate has most definitely reached burnout and the Universe had told her it was time to stop wasting time and follow her dreams and inner calling.

Kate worked hard to get her physical and mental strength back, going from not being able to walk around the garden without struggling to climbing Snowdon a few years later, all whilst serving so many amazing clients and helping them go from their Hamster Wheel to Happiness via her company My Natural Happiness and her programmes within.

Kate realised that no matter how much work was done on the outer level, time and time again, especially for the Women who chose to work with her, that it was the inner level that had so many layers and blockages to be cleared.

So very often it was the shackles of the past holding these amazing, incredible Women from being seen and heard in this lifetime – so very past lifetimes of fear of being tortured and burnt at the stake stopped them from unfurling their wings to be seen and heard in this lifetime – and so, after a lifetime of doing deep inner, spiritual work for herself she began to share these learnings with her clients – and the results were incredible.

Kate was inspired to help as many amazing incredible Women as is possible Shine their Lights so brightly, in order to help bring some wonderful balance to the Patriarchal society we live in, balance which can only be a good thing going forward – Kate feels that this is a life calling to publish this book and hopes that you enjoy the book as you work through the book.

Find out more about Kate at www.mynaturalhappiness.com

QR code for website:

And www.magicalcourses.mynaturalhappiness.com

QR code for more courses

Printed in Great Britain
by Amazon